Frostie's

12 CRAZY DAYS OF CHRISTMAS

Every Christmas season is crazy, when you own a toy store. This story tells a tale, of when things went very wrong at Frosties Toy Store.

First there was Holly's Clinker, Clunker, Flop.

Then Mr. Cotton Puff's toy factory got all of Frosties toy orders messed up.

For every order Frosties received was wrong, when they ordered a This, instead they got a That.

With everything going so wrong, Mr. Frostie feared that there would be no toys for his customers to buy this year.

But sometimes a This, can become a That, when you change the way you see things.

Sing along and learn how Mr. Frostie made the best of everything.

FROSTIES ORDER FORM

DATE: First Day of Christmas

1. Karaoke Machine

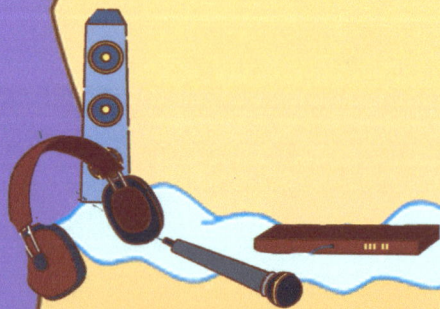

On the first day of Christmas Mr. Cotton Puff Sent to me

ONE CLAY MAKING CARROT MACHINE

FROSTIES ORDER FORM

DATE: Second Day of Christmas

2. Wolf Toys

On the second day of Christmas Mr. Cotton Puff Sent to me

FROSTIES ORDER FORM

DATE: Third Day of Christmas

3. Army Hats

On the third day of Christmas Mr. Cotton Puff Sent to me

THREE MINI ARMY FIGURES

FROSTIES ORDER FORM

DATE: Fourth Day of Christmas

4.Holiday Books

On the fourth day of Christmas Mr. Cotton Puff Sent to me

Four
Fisherman
Hooks

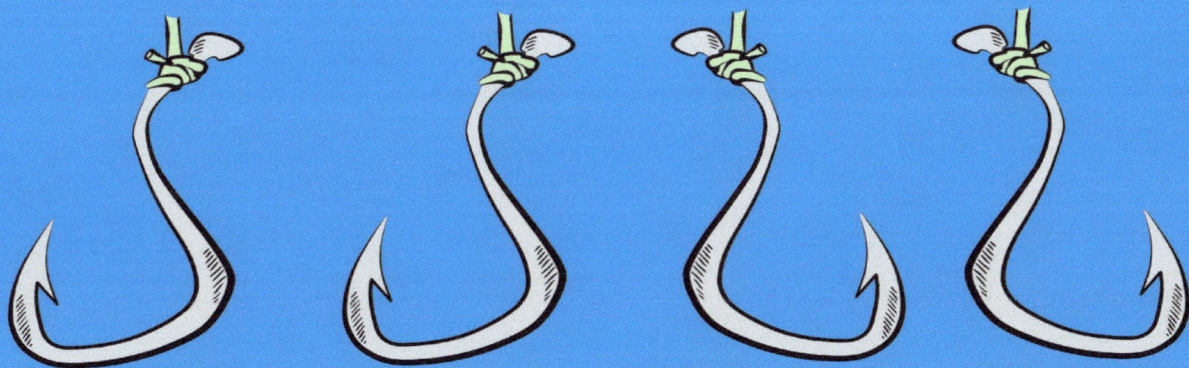

FROSTIES ORDER FORM

DATE: Fifth Day of Christmas

5. Sleds

On the fifth day of Christmas Mr. Cotton Puff Sent to me

FIVE
TRASH CAN
LIDS

FROSTIES ORDER FORM

DATE: Sixth Day of Christmas

6. Baseball Bats

On the sixth day of Christmas Mr. Cotton Puff Sent to me

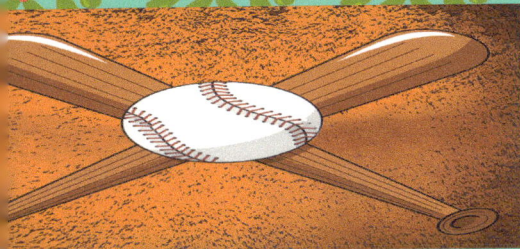

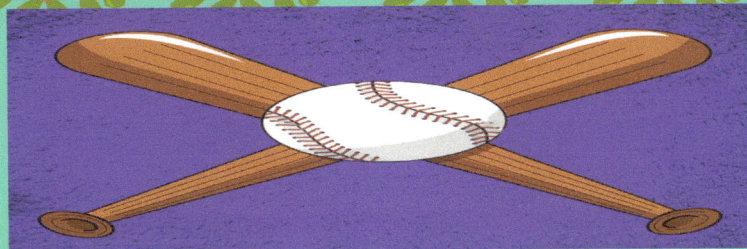

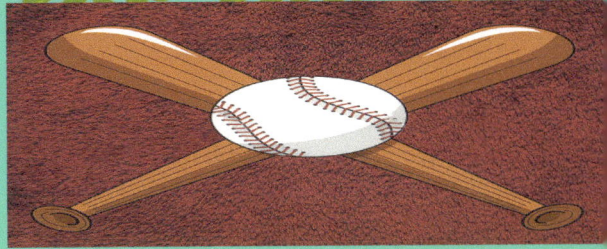

SIX
Baseball
Bathroom
Mats

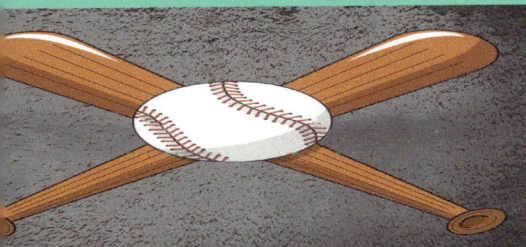

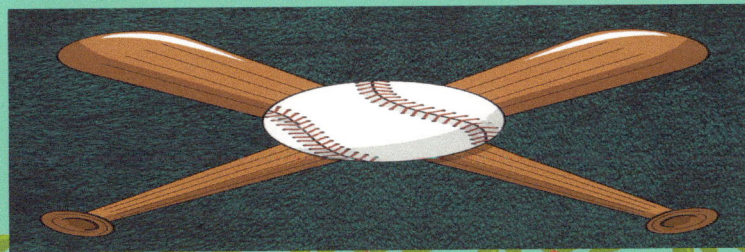

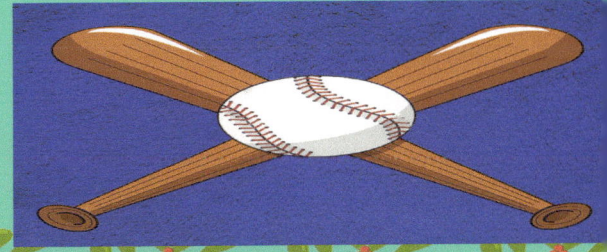

FROSTIES ORDER FORM

DATE: Seventh Day of Christmas

7. Blow up Snowman

On the seventh day of Christmas Mr. Cotton Puff Sent to me

Seven

Leprechauns

FROSTIES ORDER FORM

DATE: Eigtht Day of Christmas

8. Things of Slime

On the Eighth day of Christmas Mr. Cotton Puff Sent to me

Eight
Books of
Rhymes

Book Of Rhymes

FROSTIES ORDER FORM

DATE: Ninth Day of Christmas

9. Watermelon Squishy

On the Ninth day of Christmas Mr. Cotton Puff Sent to me

Nine Boxes of Fruit

FROSTIES ORDER FORM

DATE: Tenth Day of Christmas

10. Roller Blades

On the Tenth day of Christmas Mr. Cotton Puff Sent to me

Ten Skateboards with fan's

FROSTIES ORDER FORM

DATE: Eleventh Day of Christmas

11. Giant Christmas Bears

On the Eleventh day of Christmas Mr. Cotton Puff Sent to me

Eleven Valentine Hearts

Dasher Dancer Prancer Vixen Com

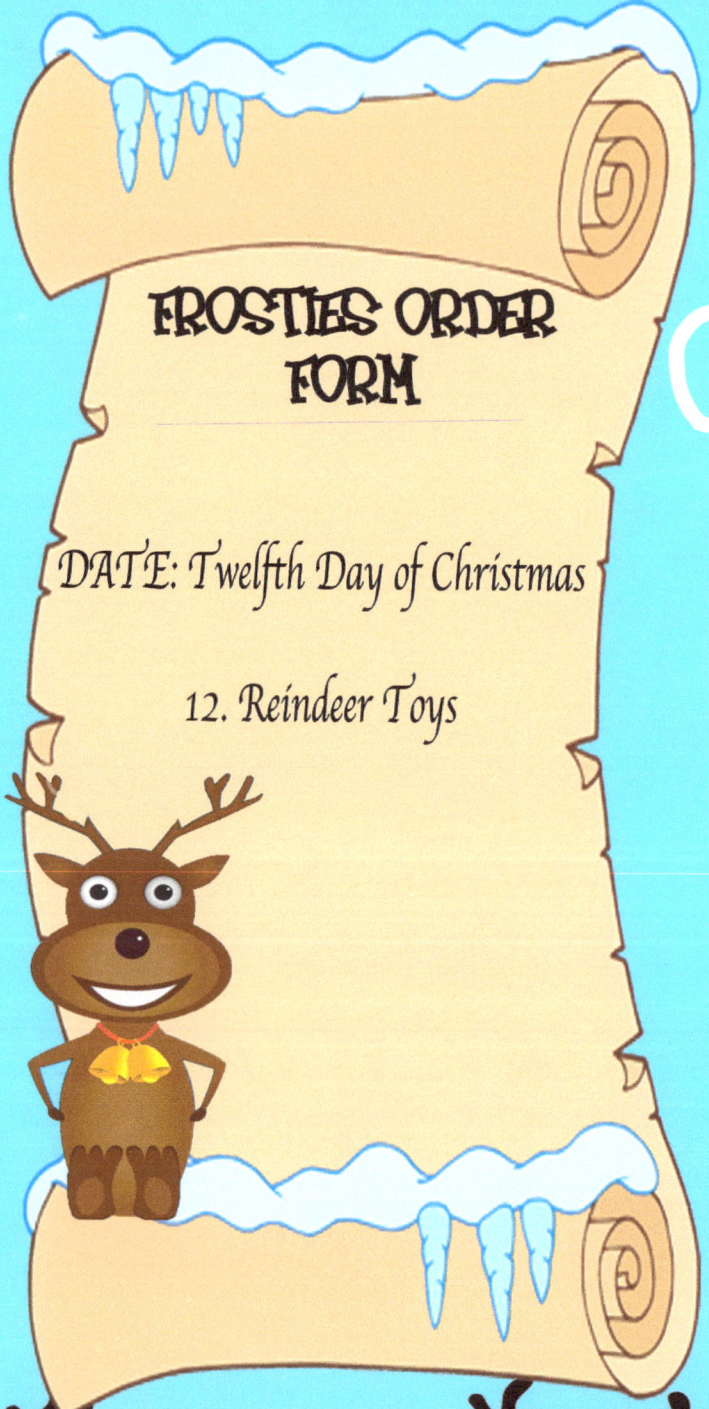

FROSTIES ORDER FORM

DATE: Twelfth Day of Christmas

12. Reindeer Toys

On the Twelfth day of Christmas Mr. Cotton Puff Sent to me

Dasher Dancer Prancer Vixen Com

Twelve Real Reindeer

One: Karaoke Machine

Two: Wolf Toys

Three: Mini Army Figures

Four: Holiday Books

Five: Sleds

Six: Baseball Bats

Seven: Blow-up Snowman

Eight: Things of Slime

Nine: Watermelon Squishy

Ten: Roller Blades

Eleven: Giant Christmas Teddy Bears

Twelve: Reindeer Toys

Contributing Authors

Julius A Loza

Lauren Muro

Cali Gutierrez

Julius A Loza: is 10 years old. He wants to be a basketball player. He enjoys playing basketball and he loves to interact with other kids. He loves to play video games and LOVES playing with Lego's. He likes to keep himself busy.

Lauren G. Muro: is 10 years old and wants to be a Dermatologist when she grows up. She loves to write, draw and play competitive soccer.

Cali Gutierrez: is 7 years old. I like to play outside. Play with my family, and my friends. I also like to play with my dogs and I have 3 dogs, one is a Husky, the other one is a German Shepard, the last one is a Collie, I almost forgot the names of the dogs. They are Lexi, Maraley, and Shadow.

Little Authors

Contributing Authors

Andrea Neira

Skylah M. Lavelle

Alexa N. Gutierrez

Andrea Neira (Tori): is 8 years old and wants to be a building designer (Architect). Her creative imagination for her short stories is out of this world!!!! They will leave you wanting more! She is very caring, loving and honest with her actions. She loves wolves, reading, and Roblox, Oh and basketball.

Skylah Marie Lavelle (Wolfie): is 11 years old and loves wolves, her puppy Coco and her adventurous life. She walks dogs, plays guitar and cooks. She is excited about middle school next year and looks forward to math, lunch and her friends. She wants to attend Texas A&M and become a Veterinarian.

Alexa N. Gutierrez: is 10 years old and wants to be a scientist when she grows up. She lo0ves to swim, play with her dog, write and read. She has three dogs named Lexi who is a 1 year old Husky, Marley who is a 1 year old German Shepard Pit-bull mix and Shadow who is a 13 year old Collie. Alexa is smart, an electronic lover and kind.

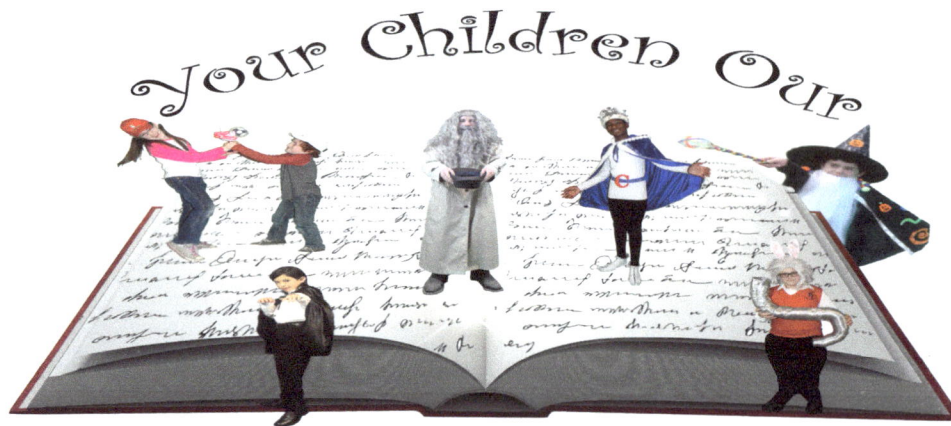

Your Children Our

Stories

CSB
INNOVATIONS

www.csbinnovations.com

www.ingramcontent.com/pod-product-compliance
Lightning Source LLC
Chambersburg PA
CBHW040404100426

42811CB00017B/1833